Original title:

Forgiving You

Author: Olivia Oja

ISBN HARDBACK: 978-9916-89-967-0

ISBN PAPERBACK: 978-9916-89-968-7

ISBN EBOOK: 978-9916-89-969-4

From Ashes to Renewal

From ashes we arise, like phoenix in the dawn,
In trials and in pain, we've been reborn.
With faith as our guide, we seek the light,
In shadows of despair, we find our might.

With each step we take, the spirit grows,
In unity we rise, through highs and lows.
The past is but dust, in the wind it flies,
For in our hearts, the promise never dies.

The Sacred Act of Letting Go

In silence we learn, to release the binds,
Like rivers flowing free, the heart unwinds.
Each burden we carry must one day cease,
In surrender we find, a sacred peace.

The weight of our grief, like leaves in the fall,
Is transformed by the winds, a gentle call.
With open hands, our souls become light,
In letting go, we embrace the night.

Flowers in a Field of Grace

In fields of grace, where the sunlight streams,
Flowers bloom in colors, like joyful dreams.
Each petal a prayer, each fragrance a song,
In nature's embrace, we all belong.

The roots intertwine, in soil so deep,
Nurtured by love, in His peace we seep.
Together we blossom, with hearts so pure,
In harmony's tune, we find our cure.

Horizons of Compassion

Beyond the mountains, where the sun meets the sky,
Lies a realm of love, where the spirits fly.
With kindness as our compass, we journey far,
Guided by the light of the evening star.

With hands open wide, we share the grace,
A tapestry of life, woven in each place.
Embracing our brothers, in joy and in strife,
In horizons of compassion, we find our life.

A Covenant of Understanding

In the stillness of the heart, we meet,
A promise whispered, sacred and sweet.
Together we tread on this path so bright,
Bound by the love that ignites the night.

Hands raised in prayer, we seek and we find,
In shared devotion, our spirits combined.
Through trials and joys, we gather as one,
A testament forged as day greets the sun.

With each shared moment, we nurture the flame,
In the sanctuary of love, we remain.
A covenant written in light and in grace,
Unified hearts, in this hallowed space.

The Grace That Frees Us

In shadows cast by burdens we bear,
A gentle whisper calls us to share.
Through trials endured, we rise and we sing,
The grace that frees us, a holy spring.

From ashes of doubt, new life is reborn,
In love's warm embrace, we are never forlorn.
Each step we take, in faith we abide,
With every heartbeat, our spirits collide.

Forgiven and loved, we walk in the light,
Casting away the dark, reclaiming our sight.
In unity bound, we journey as one,
Finding our purpose, like stars we have spun.

As the Dawn Breaks Over Us

As dawn breaks softly, shadows take flight,
Hope arises, chasing the night.
In the quiet whisper of morning’s grace,
We find the strength in a sacred space.

With each golden ray, our souls turn anew,
Embracing the promise in every hue.
Together we stand, hand in hand, we rise,
Bathed in the light that opens our eyes.

Through valleys of doubt, and mountains of fear,
We journey as pilgrims, our vision is clear.
As dawn paints the sky, we lift our hearts high,
In love's gentle warmth, our spirits comply.

In the Eye of Mercy's Storm

In the eye of a storm, we find our true peace,
A moment of stillness, a heavenly release.
When chaos surrounds, and all seems unclear,
We lean on the promise that love draws us near.

Through tempest and trial, our faith may be tried,
Yet grace is our anchor, our faithful guide.
In whispers of mercy, our fears are laid bare,
Together we rise, a community rare.

With hearts intertwined, we weather each blow,
Finding strength in each other, letting love flow.
In the eye of the storm, we stand resolute,
Rooted in faith, our spirits take root.

Redemption's Gentle Whisper

In silence, grace does dwell,
A weary soul's sweet bell.
Hearts mended with love's thread,
Darkest nights, softly sped.

Each tear a sacred gift,
In pain, our spirits lift.
Through trials, faith will bloom,
In sorrow, light breaks gloom.

With mercy's tender hand,
We rise, together stand.
Forgiven, we rejoice,
In harmony, one voice.

From ashes, new life grows,
The mercy river flows.
In trust, we find our peace,
And burdens find release.

In shadows, hope shall gleam,
We walk as if in dream.
Redemption whispers near,
Embrace the love, not fear.

In the Garden of Second Chances

Beneath the azure skies,
Grace lifts our weary sighs.
In gardens rich with bloom,
New life casts out the gloom.

Each petal tells a tale,
Where love will never fail.
In soil of faithful hearts,
Forgiveness gently starts.

The sun will greet each dawn,
With mercy gently drawn.
In every breath, a prayer,
Hope dances in the air.

Time's gentle touch will heal,
The wounds that once would steal.
We plant our seeds of grace,
In this, our sacred space.

In whispered winds, we find,
The peace that heals the mind.
In unity we grow,
Together, we bestow.

A Prayer for Unburdened Hearts

O Lord, we seek the light,
To guide us through the night.
Unburdened, let us stand,
In faith, we seek Your hand.

Release us from our fears,
Wash away our silent tears.
In Your embrace, we find,
The grace to heal the mind.

With every breath, we pray,
For strength to lead the way.
In kindness, hearts shall soar,
United evermore.

In shadows, love will shine,
With souls that intertwine.
Anointed by Your grace,
We journey to that place.

Where burdens fall away,
And night becomes the day.
In freedom, let us start,
This prayer for every heart.

The Light After Shadows

When darkness veils the way,
And hope seems far away,
The dawn will break anew,
With every shade, a hue.

In trials, truth will rise,
A beacon for our eyes.
With faith, we stand aligned,
In love, our hearts entwined.

Through storms that we endure,
Our spirits will be pure.
In every scar, a story,
That leads us to His glory.

With every rising sun,
We find what must be done.
Past shadows fade from sight,
As love reveals the light.

Together we will walk,
In grace, we softly talk.
With every step, our prayer,
The light is always there.

Rivers of Mercy Flowing

In the stillness of night, they flow,
Graceful whispers, gentle and low.
Washing wounds of the weary heart,
A divine touch that sets us apart.

From mountains high, the waters fall,
Each droplet answers a silent call.
Soothing sorrows, quenching the thirst,
In every blessing, our souls disperse.

We gather near the banks of love,
With faith as strong as wings of dove.
A sacred stream that knows no end,
In its embrace, we all transcend.

O rivers wide, with purpose so clear,
In your depths, we lose our fear.
With every tide, a rebirth is found,
In mercy's flow, our lives are bound.

Let us drink from your sacred grace,
In humble prayer, we find our place.
Together we walk, hand in hand,
Where rivers of mercy meet the land.

The Garden of Unfading Hope

In the garden where soft blooms rise,
Petals whisper underneath the skies.
Seeds of faith in darkened soil,
Nurtured with love, they toil and toil.

Sunlight kisses the earth with care,
Promises linger in fragrant air.
Roots entwined, they stand so tall,
In gentle winds, we hear the call.

Amid the thorns, our spirits soar,
With every struggle, we learn to explore.
A bloom that shines when days are dark,
In every heart, it leaves a mark.

Nurtured by tears and laughter too,
In this garden, hope shines anew.
Every season brings its chance,
In nature's grace, we find our dance.

Together we tend our sacred ground,
In silence, strength and peace abound.
The garden thrives in faith's embrace,
In unending hope, we find our place.

The Sacred Dance of Amends

In the quiet hours of the morn,
We gather voices, humbled, worn.
To mend the bonds that life has torn,
In sacred circles, we are reborn.

With gentle hearts, we take a chance,
In every step, our souls advance.
Forgiveness flows like a gentle stream,
In the dance of love, we find our dream.

Each footfall speaks of grace and care,
With open spirits, we lay our bare.
For every fault, a chance to heal,
In the rhythm of life, we learn to feel.

Hand in hand, we weave the light,
In shadows, we find the strength to fight.
The sacred dance, a balm for pain,
In unity, we rise again.

Let the music of grace resound,
In every heart, compassion found.
As we dance through night and day,
In amends, we find our way.

Pillars of Empathy and Trust

In a world where shadows creep,
Stand the pillars, strong and deep.
Built on love, they reach the sky,
Empathy's bond, a heartfelt tie.

Through trials faced and storms once braved,
In every soul, a kindness saved.
With trust as our unyielding light,
We illuminate the darkest night.

Listening hearts share the load,
In silence, love's true story flowed.
Together forging paths anew,
In every bond, our spirits grew.

Through struggles shared, we find our way,
In unity, we choose to stay.
As pillars rise against the strain,
In empathy, we break the chain.

Let every voice with purpose ring,
In harmony, a hope we bring.
With trust as roots and love as guide,
Pillars stand strong, forever wide.

Grace in the Shadows

In silence whispers grace does dwell,
A gentle touch, a sacred spell.
In darkest nights where fears ignite,
Hope's tender glow brings forth the light.

Faint echoes of a love profound,
In hidden places, faith is found.
The weary soul, though worn and frayed,
Is wrapped in mercy unafraid.

While burdens heavy loom above,
The heart can rest in endless love.
With every tear that softly falls,
The grace of God in stillness calls.

Though shadows stretch and doubts may rise,
A radiant truth beneath the skies.
Forgiveness flows like rivers wide,
In shadows deep, our hearts abide.

Together we will rise anew,
In faith's embrace, our spirits grew.
The promise made, the path so clear,
In grace, we walk, no room for fear.

Redemption’s Embrace

In every sin, a story told,
A journey lost, a heart grown cold.
Yet in the depths, a hand extends,
Redemption's love, it never bends.

Each step of faith, a dance divine,
Transformation flows like sweetened wine.
With every fall, the cycle turns,
A heart that breaks, but always yearns.

Forgiveness whispers in the night,
Restoring hope, igniting light.
What once was shattered now can mend,
In love's embrace, we start again.

The past may cling, but grace will guide,
Through trials faced, with Christ beside.
From shadows cast to dawn's embrace,
Redemption shines with boundless grace.

For every tear that we have cried,
Is but a seed for joy inside.
In trials faced, His truth will bloom,
With arms spread wide, love conquers gloom.

Beneath the Weight of Grace

In weary hearts where burdens lie,
The weight of grace will lift us high.
A gentle hand, a soft refrain,
Through storms and strife, we break the chain.

When shadows creep and fears confront,
With faith, we view the daunting front.
Each whispered prayer that leaves our lips,
Will steady hearts and calm the ships.

The grace of God, our solid ground,
Where lost and broken can be found.
With each small step, the path unfolds,
A tender love, a story bold.

The moments lost, the hope restored,
In every heart, a peace ignored.
Beneath the weight, His strength we see,
In grace, our souls are truly free.

Though trials come like waves at night,
Our spirits soar in love's pure light.
Embraced by grace, we find our place,
A testament to love's embrace.

The Light That Guides My Heart

When shadows fall and darkness reigns,
A beacon shines, erasing pains.
In stillness found, His voice, it calls,
A whisper sweet that never stalls.

With broken dreams and fear's dark shade,
The light of faith will never fade.
Each step in trust, a spark ignites,
Guiding souls through silent nights.

In gentle beams, His truth revealed,
A warmth embraced, all wounds are healed.
With love so pure, we walk the way,
In every dawn, His light will stay.

Though trials bend the fragile frame,
Our hearts ignite with love's great flame.
A guiding star, forever bright,
In every moment, He is the light.

With every breath, we sing His praise,
In joy and sorrow, hearts ablaze.
For in His love, my spirit starts,
The light of heaven guides my heart.

Embracing the Cross of Regret

In shadows deep, I walk alone,
Beneath the weight, my heart has grown.
Each step I take, a whisper calls,
Forgiveness waits beyond these walls.

The burden pressed, my spirit worn,
Yet in this pain, new hope is born.
With every tear, a lesson learned,
In love's embrace, my soul has turned.

The cross I bear, a path to grace,
In the mirror of the human face.
Through trials fierce, a faith restored,
In humble prayer, I seek the Lord.

Each morn I rise, renewed in light,
Watching dawn dispel the night.
In mercy's glow, my heart shall sing,
Of second chances, life can bring.

The River of Grace Flows On

Down the valley, waters flow,
A river pure, where kindness grows.
Each gentle wave, a sweet refrain,
Of love's embrace, in joy and pain.

The current's strong, yet soft and wise,
It carries all beneath the skies.
With every bend, new hope appears,
A symphony of faith and tears.

From rocky shores to quiet streams,
This river holds our deepest dreams.
In flowing grace, we find our way,
Awakening to a brand new day.

With open hearts, we journey forth,
Embracing the gifts of true worth.
Together, we share in love's embrace,
As the river of grace flows on with grace.

Mosaic of Healing Souls

In broken shards, we find our worth,
An artful dance upon the earth.
Each piece reflects a story told,
Of love and hope, both brave and bold.

Together we craft a vibrant scene,
Where pain can heal and hearts glean.
With every hue, a life restored,
In unity, we seek the Lord.

The colors blend in sweet embrace,
Creating beauty from each trace.
In every crack, a light does gleam,
A tapestry woven from our dream.

So let us gather, hand in hand,
Building a world where we stand.
In love's mosaic, souls intertwine,
A sacred bond, forever divine.

Beneath the Wings of Compassion

Beneath the wings that shelter all,
We find our strength when shadows call.
With gentle grace, we learn to heal,
Embracing love, our hearts reveal.

In silent prayer, we lift the weak,
Through tender words, we share the meek.
Each act of kindness, a holy vow,
In the moment's breath, we live the now.

Under the watch of skies above,
We journey forth in faith and love.
The ties we weave are pure and bright,
In unity, we share the light.

So let us stand with arms held wide,
In every soul, let hope abide.
Beneath the wings, our spirits soar,
Together, we become much more.

The Gift of Letting Go

In silent whispers, we release,
Our burdens laid, we find our peace.
The past a shadow, fading light,
In trust, we walk into the bright.

With every breath, a gift bestowed,
The weight of worries starts to erode.
We clasp our hands in hopeful grace,
And find our strength in Your embrace.

The river flows, take heart and flow,
In letting go, our spirits grow.
With each new dawn, a chance to rise,
To see the world through open eyes.

The chains of yesterday dissolve,
In faith's embrace, our souls evolve.
No longer bound by fears that bind,
In surrender, true peace we find.

So take this heart, O Divine Light,
In letting go, we reach new height.
With every step, we learn to soar,
The gift of joy, forevermore.

A Heart Renewed in Faith

In every trial, a chance to grow,
Through shadows deep, Your love will flow.
A heart once weary finds its grace,
In faith renewed, we seek Your face.

Each morning's light, a fresh embrace,
With open arms, You fill the space.
We rise anew, with hope in sight,
Guided by Your eternal light.

When storms do rage and doubts appear,
In whispered prayer, we draw You near.
Our hearts, once crushed, now beat with song,
In unity, we shall be strong.

Your promises, like seeds, will bloom,
In gardens watered, dispelling gloom.
With every trial, we learn to stand,
A heart transformed by Your gentle hand.

So let us walk this path of grace,
With faith renewed, we'll find our place.
In every moment, hold us tight,
A heart in trust, forever bright.

Beneath the Silent Altar

Beneath the silent altar's peace,
Our weary souls find sweet release.
In prayerful whispers, hearts align,
Awakening to grace divine.

The flickering flame ignites the dark,
In stillness, we feel Your holy spark.
The weight of burdens softly bared,
In sacred space, we feel You near.

The echoes of our hearts resound,
A sanctuary, love profound.
In every tear, a story shared,
The silent altar, hearts laid bare.

Embracing now, what we let go,
In trust, we see our spirits grow.
With arms outstretched to skies above,
Beneath this altar, endless love.

So may we linger, dwell in grace,
In sacred moments, find our place.
Beneath the silent altar's glow,
We meet our God, and learn to flow.

The Prayer of Release

With humble hearts, we come to pray,
As burdens heavy start to sway.
In whispered sighs, we seek the calm,
The prayer of release, a sacred psalm.

We cast our cares upon the wind,
In faith, we know our hearts shall mend.
The chains of worry fade away,
In trust, we find the light of day.

Each tear a step toward freedom's song,
In letting go, we grow so strong.
With open hands, we lift our plea,
O Lord, embrace our spirits free.

In every moment, shed the weight,
With every breath, we choose our fate.
The prayer of release, divine embrace,
In flowing love, we find our place.

So guide us, Lord, in every breath,
From life's mistakes, we seek new depth.
With hearts unbound, our worries cease,
In gentle faith, we find our peace.

The Breaking of Chains

In shadows deep, the spirit cries,
The weight of sin, it breaks and sighs.
But grace descends, a gentle hand,
Releasing hearts at His command.

The chains that bind begin to fade,
In faithfulness, our fears are laid.
With every prayer, a strength anew,
The promise shines, both bright and true.

From ashes rise, the lost find peace,
In love's embrace, all burdens cease.
A symphony of voices raise,
To hail the One who breaks the maze.

No longer slaves to dark despair,
For in His light, we find repair.
Each chain that falls, a story told,
Of mercy vast and love untold.

In freedom's dance, we lift our song,
In harmony, the weak grow strong.
For Jesus reigns, the Savior dear,
In Him, our chains disappear.

A Light in the Wilderness

In wilderness, where shadows loom,
A flicker shines, dispelling gloom.
The path ahead, though rough and wild,
Is graced by love; the heart's sweet child.

Through barren lands, His presence glows,
With every step, our courage grows.
A guiding star, in darkest night,
He leads us forth, our hope, our light.

In trials faced, we find our ground,
For in His strength, we are unbound.
Where fears may rise, He calms the sea,
With whispers soft, “Come follow Me.”

Each day anew, we seek His face,
In every step, we find His grace.
The wilderness may stretch and bend,
But with our Lord, we find our friend.

So let the light within us blaze,
In wilderness, we sing His praise.
With hearts ablaze, we walk by faith,
A light in darkness, love's embrace.

The Embrace of a Merciful Heart

In gentle whispers, mercy speaks,
A balm for souls, for weary peaks.
With open arms, He bids us come,
To find our rest, our truest home.

Forgiveness flows, like rivers wide,
In every tear, He's at our side.
The broken find a peace so rare,
In grace's hand, we lay our care.

Each stumbling step, He understands,
With every fault, He gently stands.
His kindness wraps, a warm embrace,
Transforming hurts with endless grace.

For in His heart, compassion thrives,
Where hope ignites, and love derives.
No one is lost, none left behind,
In mercy's arms, our hearts aligned.

So lift your gaze, and know you're seen,
In every shadow, love's serene.
His merciful heart, forever near,
In all our trials, He's always here.

The Altar of Forgiveness

In the stillness of the heart, we pray,
Laying burdens down, casting fears away.
A light shines bright upon the stone,
In humble grace, we find our own.

With every tear, the soul finds peace,
In this sacred space, all strife shall cease.
Cleansed by love, our spirits rise,
At the altar, we find the prize.

Whispers of mercy fill the air,
In the depths of despair, we lay bare.
Forgiveness flows like a river's song,
In unity, together, we belong.

Hearts entwined in a holy dance,
Seeking solace in divine romance.
At dawn's first light, we break the chains,
In forgiveness, healing remains.

Oh, sacred altar, where hope ignites,
In shadows cast, the heart's insight.
With every prayer, a promise is made,
In forgiveness, love shall never fade.

A Symphony of Graceful Healing

In the silence, a melody calls,
Echoing softly through sacred halls.
A symphony of peace, in gentle strain,
Healing the heart, easing the pain.

With every note, a wound is mended,
Harmony flows, and love is blended.
In the hands of grace, we find our way,
Guided by light, we shall not stray.

Whispers of truth like a songbird's flight,
In the darkest hour, we find the light.
A dance of joy in the spirit's embrace,
In the music of healing, we find our place.

Every tear falls like a sacred tune,
Underneath the watchful moon.
Together we rise, together we stand,
A symphony of hope, hand in hand.

In the stillness, let the heart rejoice,
For in healing, we hear our voice.
With faith as our guide, we shall be whole,
In a symphony of grace, we find our soul.

Threads of Redemption Woven

In the tapestry of life, we weave,
Threads of redemption that we believe.
With each heartbeat, a story unfolds,
In the fabric of faith, the truth holds.

Stitched with love and compassion's grace,
Every struggle leaves a trace.
In the loom of time, our dreams align,
Threads of hope intertwined in design.

The colors of joy amidst shadows cast,
In the present moment, we embrace the past.
With gentle hands, the touch of fate,
Woven together, we conquer hate.

In every tear, a pearl shines bright,
Threads of forgiveness weaving through the night.
As we journey forth, let us take flight,
In redemption's embrace, we'll find the light.

Oh, sacred fabric, rich in grace,
With every thread, we find our place.
In unity, our spirits rise,
Threads of redemption, under open skies.

The Dawn After Darkness

In the silence of night, hope is born,
As stars whisper softly, the world is worn.
Yet deep in shadows, the promise shines,
A dawn will break, where love entwines.

With every heartbeat, the light grows bright,
Chasing the demons that haunt the night.
In the tender glow, we find our way,
A fresh new start at the break of day.

Through trials faced, the soul grows strong,
In the quiet dawn, we sing our song.
Fear gives way to a radiant grace,
In the warm embrace of this sacred space.

As the sun ascends, darkness recedes,
In the heart of each soul, a garden seeds.
With faith as our guide, we rise and stand,
In the dawn after darkness, hand in hand.

Rejoice, oh heart, for the day is new,
In light's embrace, we start anew.
With courage ablaze, we take our flight,
For the dawn after darkness brings hope's light.

The Echo of Compassionate Souls

In the silence of the night, they weep,
Hearts echoing love, promises deep.
A gentle light shines in their eyes,
Compassion flows, where mercy lies.

Hands lifted high, in fervent prayer,
Soft whispers of hope fill the air.
Together they stand, united and strong,
In the embrace of grace, they belong.

Lifting the fallen, healing the blind,
In service to others, true joy they find.
With every act, their spirits soar,
In the echo of kindness, forevermore.

Through trials and storms, they shall tread,
Following the path that love has led.
With every heartbeat, a timeless call,
They rise and unite, compassion for all.

From ashes to life, they bring the flame,
In the garden of faith, they shall reclaim.
With every breath, their voices entwine,
The echo of souls, divine and sublime.

Under the Blessings of Redemption

In shadows once cast, a light breaks through,
The promise of grace, forever true.
Chains are unbound, spirits set free,
Under redemption's wings, we shall be.

With every step, the past fades away,
Hope paints the skies at the dawn of day.
In the warmth of forgiveness, we can grow,
The seeds of love blossom, restoring the flow.

A journey begins, hand in hand,
Together we rise, united we stand.
Through valleys of doubt, we'll walk as one,
Under the blessings of the Holy Son.

In the crumbling ruins, new life shall emerge,
The river of mercy flows with a surge.
Each tear that falls, a sign of the heart,
From brokenness, we'll craft a new start.

As sunlight breaks forth, the night fades away,
In the promise of dawn, we find our way.
With faith as our banner, in love we shall tread,
Under the blessings of redemption, we're led.

The Waters of Grace Cascade

From mountains high, pure waters flow,
Rivers of grace, with gentle glow.
They nourish the weary, the lost, the meek,
In every droplet, love does speak.

Cascading softly, soothing the land,
Healing the broken, lending a hand.
In deep pools of faith, we seek to drink,
With every sip, our spirits link.

The waterfalls roar, a heavenly song,
As heartbeats align, where we belong.
Riding the currents of soulful care,
In the waters of grace, find peace in prayer.

Beneath the surface, treasures lie deep,
Secrets of wisdom, for souls to keep.
Each wave that crashes, a reminder of light,
In the depths of despair, faith ignites the night.

As we dive deeper, our fears erase,
In the arms of mercy, we find our place.
Forever transformed, a beautiful mask,
In the waters of grace, let love be our task.

Rebuilding the Temple of Trust

With stones of truth, we lay the ground,
In the sacred realm, where love is found.
Brick by brick, our hearts we mend,
Rebuilding the temple, where souls transcend.

Through trials faced, our faith will stand,
Hand in hand, we’re led by the hand.
In moments of doubt, we'll rise above,
In the temple of trust, we'll build with love.

The echoes of laughter, the warmth of grace,
In every corner, joy finds a place.
We gather together, with spirits aglow,
In unity we flourish, as light starts to grow.

With prayers as beams, and hope as our roof,
The sanctuary of trust, stands proud and aloof.
In the shadows of doubt, we’ll shine so bright,
Rebuilding our souls in the purest light.

From ashes to beauty, we’ll raise our voice,
In the heart of the temple, our spirits rejoice.
With faith as our guide, love holds us tight,
Rebuilding the temple, in trust, we unite.

A Symphony of Graceful Hearts

In the stillness, praises rise,
Hearts entwined under the skies.
Harmony flows like rivers free,
Each note a whisper, a sacred plea.

With every beat, a love so grand,
Guiding us by His gentle hand.
Unity in grace we find,
In every heart, a love defined.

Through trials faced and storms we brave,
Together we dance, our souls we save.
In the chorus of faith, we stand,
Echoing truths across the land.

Let kindness reign, let mercy flow,
A symphony of hearts aglow.
With every breath, we'll sing our part,
A melody born from a graceful heart.

In the twilight, when shadows play,
Hope flickers bright, lighting the way.
Together we'll rise, hope's resound,
In this symphony, love is found.

A Tapestry of Redeeming Love

Threads of grace weave through time,
Bound together, a sacred rhyme.
Each knot a story, each color a tear,
A tapestry of love drawing near.

In moments broken, we find the light,
Guided by faith through the darkest night.
With every stitch, a promise made,
In love's embrace, our fears will fade.

Every life, a unique strand,
Woven together by a divine hand.
Through trials and triumphs, we come to know,
The beauty that through struggle can grow.

In every pattern, a purpose shines,
A tribute to love, where grace aligns.
Together we craft, hand in hand,
A masterpiece across the land.

Whispering prayers in silence deep,
The tapestry of hearts we keep.
In its warmth, we find our place,
A testament to redeeming grace.

Gifts of Compassionate Grace

In gentle hands, grace is found,
A gift of love, profound and sound.
With every act, a heart does heal,
In compassion's light, our souls reveal.

Through weary eyes, we see the pain,
Yet in our bonds, hope will remain.
With kindness shared, we lift the weak,
In every word, the Savior speaks.

Compassion flows like rivers wide,
A boundless tide, a sacred guide.
In caring hearts, we find our way,
A light to brighten the darkest day.

Each moment offers a chance to give,
In grace we learn just how to live.
With every gift, a loving trace,
Together we grow in compassionate grace.

United in spirit, we rise as one,
Our journey steadfast, never done.
Let kindness reign, let love embrace,
The world transformed through compassionate grace.

A Song for Every Wounded Heart

In silence deep, a song takes flight,
A melody born from darkest night.
With every tear, a note will play,
A balm of love to light the way.

For every soul that bears a scar,
Hope whispers soft, 'You’re never far.'
In troubled times, the chords resound,
A healing hymn where grace is found.

Lift up your voice, let love impart,
Each word a thread to bind the heart.
With every sound, a spirit healed,
In songs of faith, our wounds revealed.

Through valleys low and mountains tall,
A chorus rises, a sweetened call.
A hymn of strength to mend the brave,
For wounded hearts, His love will save.

In the twilight, when shadows part,
Find peace within, a tender start.
For in this song, we all take part,
A symphony for every wounded heart.

The Anchor of Forgiveness

In shadows deep, we find our grace,
A gentle heart, a warm embrace.
With open palms, the burden fades,
A light within, where love invades.

Each whispered prayer, a soothing balm,
In storms of life, we seek the calm.
Forgiving souls, we rise anew,
In faith's sweet light, our spirits grew.

The anchor holds, through trials near,
In tender mercy, lose all fear.
A tapestry of hope we weave,
In every heart, we learn to believe.

Embracing faults, we walk the road,
In unity, we share the load.
With every step, we grow in love,
Guided by grace from above.

When Spirits Dance in Unity

In sacred circles, hearts entwined,
We join our voices, intertwined.
With every beat, the rhythm flows,
In harmony, our spirit grows.

The light of grace, a guiding star,
Illuminates our path from far.
We lift our hands, embrace the night,
In unity, our souls take flight.

With open hearts, we find the way,
In laughter shared, in joy's display.
Each gesture kind, a dance divine,
Together here, our spirits shine.

In sacred moments, time stands still,
With every heartbeat, love we fill.
As whispers weave a tender song,
In unity, we all belong.

A Symphony of Healing Hearts

In quiet corners, healing starts,
With gentle words, we mend our hearts.
Each note we play, a sacred sound,
In every soul, compassion found.

Resilient love, a guiding light,
Through darkest days, we seek the bright.
With every tear, a strength unfolds,
In tender moments, courage molds.

Together we rise, hand in hand,
A symphony, we bravely stand.
With every hymn, a bond of grace,
In this embrace, we find our place.

Each story told, a truth revealed,
In shared embrace, our wounds are healed.
With hearts as one, we sing anew,
In unity, our love shines through.

The Echoes of Compassionate Souls

In gentle whispers, hearts collide,
With every echo, love's our guide.
Compassion flows like a river wide,
In every soul, we do confide.

Through trials faced and burdens shared,
With open arms, we're always paired.
In kindness found, our spirits soar,
An endless grace, forevermore.

Each act of love, a seed we sow,
In tender fields where hope can grow.
With every step, we find our role,
In harmony, we heal the soul.

Across the ages, stories speak,
Of love's embrace in times so bleak.
The echoes ring, a timeless song,
In compassionate hearts, we belong.

Love’s Unbroken Promise

In the light of dawn we seek,
A whisper divine, gentle and meek.
In every heart, His grace does flow,
Binding souls with love aglow.

Through valleys deep, through shadows cast,
His promises remain, unbroken, steadfast.
With every trial, with every tear,
His presence assures, forever near.

In the silence, a sacred vow,
To lift the weary, to teach us how.
A covenant made, in faith we stand,
Walking together, hand in hand.

The storms may rage, the winds may wail,
Yet love endures, it shall not fail.
For in each heartbeat, a truth we find,
Love's unbroken promise, forever intertwined.

So let us sing, let our voices rise,
To the heavens above, where love never dies.
In every moment, let His light shine,
Love’s unbroken promise, eternally divine.

The Serpent and the Dove

Amidst the whispers of night so still,
The serpent lurks, with cunning, ill will.
Yet the dove, so pure, takes to the sky,
In faith unwavering, it learns to fly.

In shadows of doubt, the heart may roam,
But the spirit finds solace, returns to home.
With wisdom of ages, the truth will sway,
The serpent will fade, but the dove shall stay.

In trials faced, with courage we stand,
For peace and love are always at hand.
With eyes open wide, and hearts ablaze,
We rise above, in sacred praise.

For every conflict brings lessons learned,
In the balance of love, our hearts are turned.
With grace to forgive, and strength to unite,
The serpent retreats, engulfed by the light.

So let us embrace, both night and day,
For in every struggle, we find our way.
With the dove leading forth, in grace we trust,
In the dance of life, it's love, not lust.

Weaving Threads of Kindness

In the tapestry of life, threads intertwine,
Each act of kindness, a design so fine.
With gentle hands, we sow the seeds,
Of compassion and love, fulfilling needs.

A smile shared, a listening ear,
Can change a heart, can bring us near.
With every gesture, great and small,
We cast the net of love for all.

Through trials faced and burdens borne,
A web of kindness helps us not to mourn.
With every thread, a story told,
A legacy of love, more precious than gold.

In unity we stand, diverse yet one,
Our hearts ablaze, like the morning sun.
We weave together, each soul alike,
In the grand design, our spirits strike.

So let us fashion, with care and grace,
A world transformed, a sacred space.
For in kindness shared, we truly find,
The bond that lifts, that blesses mankind.

Hearts Born Again Within His Love

In the stillness of night, the spirit ignites,
Hearts born again, reaching new heights.
With every prayer, a flame does burn,
A journey of faith, for which we yearn.

In the depths of despair, grace flows free,
Healing the wounds of iniquity.
With arms wide open, He welcomes us near,
In His love, we shed every fear.

From ashes to beauty, the past unveils,
In love's embrace, the heart prevails.
With every heartbeat, redemption sings,
New life awakens, on faith's great wings.

In joy we gather, His children unite,
With purpose renewed, we walk in the light.
For every tear shed, a seed is sown,
Hearts born again, forever His own.

So let us rejoice, in love ever true,
For in His heart, we’re always made new.
With each step forward, let us proclaim,
Hearts born again, forever the same.

The Touch of Divine Mercy

In shadows deep, His light will break,
With gentle hands, our hearts He'll wake.
Through weary nights, a soft refrain,
His mercy flows, erasing pain.

In every tear, a promise stands,
Restoration comes from loving hands.
He whispers hope in darkest days,
To lost souls wandering in the maze.

Upon our brows, He lays His peace,
In silent prayer, our burdens cease.
The touch of grace, a sacred sign,
In every heart, His love will shine.

When struggles rise like stormy seas,
His presence calms; our spirits ease.
In faith we trust, and never stray,
For in His arms, we're led each day.

Hope Through the Veil of Sorrow

When shadows loom and spirits fade,
Hope flickers dim, yet softly stayed.
Through trials faced, the heart will learn,
In every pain, love's flame will burn.

Each tear we shed, a seed is sown,
From grief, new strength shall be grown.
The veil of sorrow, sheer yet thin,
Holds hidden grace that waits within.

In moments lost, His light will gleam,
Unfolding dreams that still redeem.
Though weary paths may drain our soul,
Hope’s gentle whisper makes us whole.

So lift your eyes, see stars above,
Each shining point, a sign of love.
Through struggle’s grip, we rise and stand,
In faith united, hand in hand.

The Language of Healing Hearts

In silence shared, our spirits speak,
With kindness found in every leak.
The language soft, a touch so pure,
In brokenness, we find the cure.

Each word a balm, each glance a grace,
We learn to heal, our hearts embrace.
In every hug, a power grows,
A sacred bond that gently flows.

Through trials faced, we gather near,
In unity, we shed each fear.
For love unites in darkest night,
The healing song brings forth the light.

With every beat, our hearts align,
In whispered prayers, divinity shines.
The language shared, so deep and vast,
In healing hearts, forgiveness lasts.

In the Embrace of Everlasting Grace

In gentle whispers, grace will flow,
Like morning dew, it starts to grow.
Embraced by love, we find our place,
In every challenge, His warm grace.

Through every trial, a story told,
In every heart, His love unfolds.
A tryst with hope, a sacred dance,
In grace we find our second chance.

When burdens weigh and shadows loom,
His light will pierce the deepest gloom.
In trust we walk, forever strong,
In grace, we'll find where we belong.

So let us sing this heartfelt hymn,
In gratitude for love so dim.
In every breath, His warmth we trace,
Forever held in endless grace.

A Journey Back to the Light

In shadows deep, we seek the dawn,
With faith as our guide, we carry on.
Each step we take, a whispered prayer,
In the warm embrace of love, we share.

Through valleys low, the path may wind,
Yet in each heart, true peace we find.
With every trial, our spirits rise,
Towards higher realms, beneath vast skies.

The sun will shine, dispelling fears,
As grace collects the scattered tears.
In unity, our voices blend,
A journey bright, with God, our friend.

So trust the light, its gentle glow,
It leads us forth, to know and grow.
In every heartbeat, a sacred spark,
Illuminates the boundless dark.

The Blossoming of a Trusting Heart

A seed of faith, within us lies,
To nourish love, it slowly tries.
With tender care, we watch it bloom,
Transforming fears that once brought gloom.

In gentle whispers, hope abounds,
As grace and beauty in us resound.
With open arms, we greet the day,
In trusting hearts, we find our way.

Let kindness flow, a river wide,
To heal the wounds we often hide.
As petals dance in the softest breeze,
True joy emerges, a life of ease.

Through every storm, our roots run deep,
In sacred moments, dreams we keep.
A trusting heart, forever bright,
Shall guide our souls back to the light.

Reflections in the Waters of Grace

In still waters, the heavens meet,
A mirrored heart, pure and complete.
With ripples soft, our souls align,
Reflecting love, divine, benign.

Each glance reveals the truth so clear,
As grace awakens every fear.
In quietude, we hear the call,
To rise together, we shall not fall.

The waters sing of love unbound,
In every drop, His presence found.
We drink of peace, our spirits soar,
In sacred silence, we explore.

Through trials faced, we find the way,
Guided by light, come what may.
With grateful hearts, we bear the trace,
Of holy whispers, in this grace.

Tides of Kindness

In the ocean's flow, we find our place,
Tides of kindness, a warm embrace.
With waves of love, our spirits lift,
Creating bonds, a treasured gift.

Each ripple spreads, touching souls near,
In acts of grace, we cast out fear.
Through giving hearts, the world will see,
The beauty held in unity.

Let compassion rain, like gentle drops,
In every heart, the love never stops.
As seasons change, our roots hold fast,
In kinder deeds, the future's cast.

Through every storm and darkest night,
The tide of kindness brings forth light.
With open hands, we shall bestow,
The love that flourishes, like springtime's glow.

Rising Above the Ruins

In ashes deep where shadows fade,
A beacon shines, a hope displayed.
From broken ground, new dreams arise,
With faith as wings, we touch the skies.

Each step we take, a prayer we weave,
In unity, we still believe.
The past may haunt, yet love will guide,
Together strong, we shall abide.

The whispers of the lost and gone,
Remind us of the dawn's new song.
With every heartbeat, grace restores,
As we ascend to distant shores.

From rubble springs a life renewed,
In trials faced, our spirits stewed.
Through every storm, our hearts unite,
In struggles found, we seek the light.

So let us rise, though shadows loom,
In sacred strength, dispel the gloom.
With open hearts and hands held tight,
We'll build again; we'll shine so bright.

The Flame of New Beginnings

In darkness deep, a flicker glows,
A spark ignites, as courage grows.
From past's despair, a fire ignites,
With every breath, we claim new heights.

Let doubts dissolve like morning mist,
Embrace the light, our path persist.
In whispered prayers, we find a way,
To rise anew with every day.

The flame of faith will light the night,
Each trembling heart, a guiding light.
In unity, our voices sing,
A sacred bond, this hope we bring.

With every flicker, shadows flee,
Resilience blooms from love set free.
In trials faced, our spirits soared,
A tapestry of grace restored.

So let the flames of hope ascend,
In every heart, we will transcend.
With love's embrace, our lives will shine,
A story told through time divine.

In the Heart of Compassionate Grace

Amidst the storms, where kindness flows,
The heart of grace in silence grows.
With open arms, we dare to stand,
To heal the wounds with gentle hands.

In every tear, a lesson learned,
Through pain we share, compassion burns.
With tender minds and spirits pure,
We seek to lift, to help, to cure.

In quiet moments, love's embrace,
A sacred dance, a holy space.
Where every voice can find its song,
In the heart of grace, we all belong.

Together strong, we break the chains,
In unity, the world regains.
With hearts aligned and kindness spread,
Compassion blooms in words unsaid.

So let us walk this path of light,
With faith in love, we'll end the night.
In every step, let grace be seen,
A testament to what can be.

Seeds of Peace in the Soil of Regret

In shadows cast by choices made,
Regret may linger, yet hope won't fade.
With tender hands, we sow anew,
In sacred soil, where love breaks through.

Each seed we plant, a chance to grow,
Where hearts once heavy, now overflow.
In gentle whispers, healing starts,
The promise made to fragile hearts.

In every tear that falls like rain,
Resilience blooms beneath the pain.
The soil enriched by lessons learned,
In time's embrace, a love returned.

So let us cherish every root,
In fields of light, new paths we'll shoot.
With unity, our voices rise,
In harmony, we'll reach the skies.

From every sorrow, peace takes flight,
In vibrant colors, hearts unite.
With faith we plant, together mend,
In seeds of love, our journey blends.

The Tenderness of Spiritual Rebirth

In the quiet dawn's embrace,
A spirit stirs with gentle grace.
Casting off the chains of night,
We awaken to the light.

Hearts once heavy, now take flight,
In the warmth of love's pure light.
Tender whispers guide the way,
To a brighter, blessed day.

Rivers flow with healing streams,
Cleansing souls of broken dreams.
In the hush, a promise sings,
In rebirth, our spirit brings.

Hope ignites in every heart,
From the past, we now depart.
With each step, our burdens fade,
In this journey, love is made.

Beneath the stars, we come alive,
In the essence, we will thrive.
Together in this sacred space,
We find our true, divine embrace.

A Lamb's Call for Peace

In fields of green, the lamb does bleat,
A message soft, yet strong and sweet.
With each cry, a prayer does rise,
A longing for peace under the skies.

Gentle breeze that sweeps the land,
Calls for unity, heart in hand.
Woolly coat, a shield of grace,
Wrapping all in a warm embrace.

Follow the path that love has made,
Let kindness in our hearts invade.
For in each step, the world can see,
The light that shines, pure harmony.

From mountains high to valleys low,
A ripple spreads, we all can grow.
Sow the seeds of peace and care,
In every heart, let love declare.

The lamb's soft voice, a guiding star,
Leads us home, no matter how far.
In the silence, hear the call,
Together we rise, together we fall.

The Path Worn Soft by Understanding

Along the path, our footsteps tread,
In every word, the wisdom spread.
Soft and safe, the journey flows,
With open hearts, true love grows.

In the quiet, voices blend,
Sharing truths that transcend.
Empathy and grace entwined,
In this sacred space, we find.

Through listening, our souls align,
In every story, ties divine.
With each step, we learn anew,
Understanding binds me and you.

The sun sets low, yet hope ignites,
With gentle hands, we brave new heights.
In the warmth of shared embrace,
Together, we find our place.

Hearts expanded, minds now free,
In the dance of unity.
The path we walk, a wondrous song,
To understanding, we all belong.

A Benevolent Grace

In the still of the night, a whisper low,
Benevolent grace begins to flow.
With open arms, the heart receives,
A sacred love that never leaves.

Through trials faced and valleys deep,
In every moment, blessings seep.
Grace unravels like a gentle thread,
Weaving hope where shadows tread.

In kindness shared, the soul takes flight,
Each act of love ignites the light.
With hands uplifted in humble praise,
We gather strength in grace's ways.

As nature blooms in vibrant hue,
So too does grace renew the view.
From every corner, every place,
Together, we dance in belovèd grace.

As dawn breaks fair upon the hill,
We trust in grace, and it fulfills.
In every heartbeat, love's embrace,
Forever held in benevolent grace.

The Phoenix of Reconciliation

From ashes rises hope anew,
Hearts once tarnished, now break through.
Forgiveness whispers soft and clear,
In shadows cast, we draw near.

The flame that burns, a sacred guide,
In unity, we do abide.
With open arms, we share our plight,
And soar like birds into the light.

In every struggle, grace bestowed,
Through trials faced, love's fire glowed.
A phoenix born from pain and strife,
In reconciliation, we find life.

Together forged, our spirits free,
In harmony, our unity.
A tapestry, rich and divine,
In faith and love, our souls entwine.

Let every heart be light and whole,
In shared embrace, we heal the soul.
For in our journey, hand in hand,
The phoenix sings of love so grand.

A Tapestry of Love and Healing

Threads of compassion weave the day,
In every heart, love finds a way.
Wounds transformed by gentle hands,
In unity, our spirit stands.

Through every shadow, we will tread,
With faith to guide, where angels led.
And in our laughter, grace will shine,
For love's embrace is pure, divine.

In gentle whispers, healing flows,
A garden where the spirit grows.
Each broken piece brings strength anew,
In sacred trust, we weave what's true.

Hearts open wide, like flowers bloom,
In light of love, we cast out gloom.
A tapestry of souls combined,
In healing's grace, our hearts aligned.

Together we rise, hand in hand,
In the dance of life, we take a stand.
A journey made with strength and care,
In woven riches, love we share.

Echoes of Graceful Unity

In echoes soft, we find our song,
Together, where we all belong.
With every note, the spirit sings,
In timeless dance, hope's blessing brings.

Hands joined in faith, we walk as one,
With love's warm light, our journey begun.
Through trials faced, we hold so tight,
In grace we stand, with hearts alight.

United voices, strong and clear,
Together we rise, casting out fear.
Every wound healed with gentle touch,
In the depth of love, we learn so much.

In service given, spirits bright,
We are the flame, igniting light.
In every gesture, truth shall flow,
In echoes of love, together we'll grow.

The bridge of faith connects our souls,
In unity's embrace, we are made whole.
Bound by the grace that lights our way,
In every heart, love's echo stay.

The Light of a Renewed Covenant

In sacred promise, hope restored,
A light that shines, our hearts adored.
Together we gather, hand in hand,
In faith we rise, together we stand.

The dawn awakens, visions clear,
Each step we take, love draws us near.
Through storms and trials, faith will shine,
In every moment, grace divine.

With every breath, a vow we make,
To cherish peace, for love’s sweet sake.
In joy and sorrow, strength we find,
In every heart, a love entwined.

United hope, like stars aglow,
In harmony, our spirits flow.
The light of truth, our guiding star,
In shared reflection, wherever we are.

With open hearts, we bless this day,
In renewed covenant, we find our way.
For in His light, our path is true,
In love's embrace, we are renewed.

The Sacred Threads of Connection

In the tapestry of grace we weave,
Threads of hope in each heart believe.
United spirits, lifting our prayer,
In sacred love, we find our care.

Binding us close in the holy light,
Our souls entwined, shining so bright.
With every heartbeat, we come alive,
In this communion, we truly thrive.

Through trials faced and shadows cast,
In His embrace, we stand steadfast.
A thread of mercy, a bond so pure,
In love's embrace, our souls endure.

Across the ages, a whisper flows,
In every prayer, a promise glows.
Though storms may rage, we will recall,
Together we rise, united we'll stand tall.

In every tear and every smile,
His love connects us, mile by mile.
In the sacred threads, we find our way,
Together in faith, we'll never stray.

Embracing Our Shared Fallenness

We walk this path of weary days,
With heavy hearts, we seek His ways.
In our weakness, grace we find,
Embracing love that's so kind.

Together we share our burdens borne,
In broken places, hope is torn.
Yet in our flaws, humanity shows,
A glimpse of grace, where mercy flows.

Each stumble brings us to our knees,
In humility, we find release.
For fallen souls, redemption's near,
In His embrace, we shed our fear.

The mirror holds our scars and pain,
Reflections of love amidst the strain.
In shared fallenness, we arise,
Together we'll soar, beneath vast skies.

In the shadows, our spirits blend,
In unity, our hearts transcend.
With open arms, we dare to dream,
In every tear, we find the gleam.

The Feast of Second Chances

Gather 'round the table of grace,
Where broken hearts find their place.
In every morsel, healing flows,
A feast of love where kindness grows.

With humbled souls, we come anew,
Each shared moment, a vibrant hue.
In the presence of the divine call,
We rise together, united not small.

The old must go, the new will bloom,
In the light of love, banishing gloom.
A banquet set for hearts that yearn,
In every blessing, we shall learn.

With open hands and grateful sighs,
Our spirits lift, reaching the skies.
Second chances, a divine embrace,
In this feast, we find our place.

So let us dine with joy and trust,
In every bite, a promise robust.
For love's renewal, let us partake,
In the grace of second chances, awake.

A Requiem for Heavy Hearts

In the silence where sorrows dwell,
A requiem sings, a mournful bell.
Heavy hearts with burdens to bear,
In whispered prayers, we learn to care.

Echoes of troubles cloud the night,
Yet in the dark, we seek the light.
With every tear, a story's told,
In the depths, our souls unfold.

Gathered here, we mourn the pain,
In community, hope remains.
For every loss, a love remains,
A sacred bond that still sustains.

With softened hearts, we lift the plea,
For healing hands and spirits free.
In the requiem, we find our grace,
Embracing love in this sacred space.

So let the music softly play,
Guide us through the shadowed way.
For heavy hearts will find their rest,
In love's embrace, we are truly blessed.

United in the Spirit of Compassion

In the light of grace we stand,
Hearts entwined, hand in hand.
Bearing burdens, seeking peace,
In love's embrace, sorrows cease.

Voices lift in joyful song,
Together where we all belong.
Compassion's flame ignites the night,
Guiding souls with gentle light.

Through every trial, pain, and loss,
We find our strength through love's great cross.
In unity, we share the load,
A path of kindness, love bestowed.

Faith in action, we will show,
In every heart, compassion grow.
For in serving one another,
We rediscover, sister, brother.

Together we will rise and heal,
With every act, the truth we feel.
In every smile, in every touch,
The Spirit's work unfolds so much.

The Prayerful Journey Home

On the road less traveled wide,
In prayer, we find our guide.
Each step whispers of His grace,
Leading us to our embrace.

With humble hearts, we seek the light,
In shadows, He renews our sight.
Trusting in the path we roam,
In each heartbeat, we come home.

Through valleys low and mountains high,
In praises, we lift our cry.
Every pebble, every stone,
Marks the journey we have known.

In stillness, hearts begin to see,
The sacredness of being free.
Walking onward, hand in hand,
In faith, together we will stand.

Gentle winds through whispering trees,
Remind us of His loving ease.
As we gather, souls unite,
In prayer, we find our light.

Love Spawned from Ashes

From the depths of darkest night,
Hope is born, a spark of light.
In the ruins of our pain,
Love emerges, pure, unfeigned.

With faith's embrace, we rise anew,
Each scar a testament so true.
Through the fire, we found our way,
In love's dance, we choose to stay.

A fragrant bloom from ashes sprouted,
Whispers soft where once we doubted.
In every tear, a promise made,
In brokenness, His love conveyed.

Though storms may rage and shadows fall,
In unity, we hear the call.
A journey shared, we stand as one,
Through darkest skies, His will be done.

From love's ashes, strength reborn,
In the dawn, a new hope sworn.
Together, we shall boldly tread,
With love as light, where we are led.

A Pilgrimage to Restored Trust

In every step of faith we take,
We mend the bonds that once would break.
Through trials faced, we learn to see,
The beauty found in unity.

With open hearts and hands held high,
In trust, we soar, in peace we fly.
Every moment, a chance reset,
In love's embrace, our fears offset.

On winding paths, we journey far,
Each whisper leads, a guiding star.
With courage drawn from love within,
We find our strength, and hope begins.

Together, we unravel pain,
And in forgiving, we regain.
A pilgrimage to grace restored,
In every prayer, our hearts afford.

As seasons change and flowers bloom,
Trust blossoms, dispelling gloom.
In this journey, hand in hand,
We cultivate the promised land.

The Lotus in the Mud

In the depths where shadows play,
A flower blooms, facing the day.
Through the muck, it finds the light,
Its beauty shines, a pure delight.

Each petal whispers tales of grace,
Rising up from a humble place.
With every struggle, strength we find,
In the heart, love is intertwined.

So let us be like lotus fair,
Growing strong in the darkened air.
For though we crawl through life's tough grind,
In our souls, peace is defined.

The mud may cling, yet we will rise,
To meet the dawn, to touch the skies.
In faith, we stand, the world we'll greet,
With open hearts and willing feet.

Thus life unfolds, a sacred quest,
In every trial, our hearts are blessed.
A lotus born from trials endured,
In love's embrace, we are assured.

The Covenant of Kind Souls

In silence shared, our spirits bond,
Through acts of love, of which we're fond.
With gentle hands, we heal the strife,
In every heart, we sow new life.

Together we stand, a woven thread,
In kindness sown, deep words unsaid.
With eyes that see, we understand,
The power of love's guiding hand.

Each deed we do, a shining star,
Reminding us just who we are.
In each embrace, a promise made,
A light of hope will never fade.

Through trials faced, through storms we bear,
United hearts, our burdens share.
In every tear, in every cheer,
The covenant grows, sincere and clear.

Let kindness bloom in every soul,
A sacred bond that makes us whole.
With hearts aligned, we find our way,
In love's embrace, we choose to stay.

Beneath the Burden of Our Past

In shadows cast by yesterdays,
We linger long in weary ways.
With heavy hearts, we feel the weight,
Yet hope ignites a brighter fate.

Each scar we bear tells stories true,
In darkness form, the light breaks through.
With every step, we seek to find,
Forgiveness born of heart and mind.

And in the silence, whispers rise,
A prayer for peace beneath the skies.
Through pain and joy, through loss and gain,
We rise anew from every pain.

Let not our past define our way,
With every dawn, a new display.
In love we trust, in grace we stand,
Together healing, hand in hand.

So lift your head, embrace the grace,
For in our hearts, the light takes place.
Beneath our burdens, hope will soar,
In the depths of love, we find encore.

The Stillness of a Forgiven Heart

In quietude, the spirit bends,
Where love begins and never ends.
With gentle thoughts, we set things right,
In stillness found, there's purest light.

Forgiveness flows like river's stream,
Cleansing souls, fulfilling dream.
In every moment, grace unfolds,
A tapestry of love that holds.

Through trials faced, we learn to see,
The beauty in humility.
With open minds, we find our way,
In stillness, night transforms to day.

Let go the chains that bind our heart,
Embrace the love that plays its part.
In quiet depths, we find our peace,
A stillness where our worries cease.

Thus in the silence, joy is birthed,
A cherished gift of endless worth.
For in the calm, true strength we find,
The loving grace that heals the mind.

The Light Beyond the Shadows

In whispers soft, the dawn does break,
A guiding glow, for hearts awake.
Through trials dark, the soul shall rise,
In faith, behold the endless skies.

Each step we tread on holy ground,
In silent prayer, true peace is found.
With every breath, the spirit sings,
The love of God, in all things brings.

Echoes of grace, like rivers flow,
In darkest hours, the heart shall know.
A shimmer bright, through pain and fear,
The light of hope forever near.

Through shadows deep, the path is clear,
To trust in faith, to persevere.
In gentle hands, the lost are saved,
Awash in love, the heart is braved.

So lift your eyes, dear child of light,
The dawn shall come, dispelling night.
In unity, we rise anew,
A world transformed, in love's pure view.

A Sanctum of Healing

Within the silence, grace abounds,
A tender heart, where peace surrounds.
In sacred space, we find our rest,
In love divine, our souls are blessed.

With gentle hands, the healer comes,
To mend the wounds that life becomes.
In every tear, there lies a seed,
Of hope renewed, of love's great deed.

In faith we gather, hand in hand,
A circle formed upon this land.
Through trials shared, our spirits mend,
In unity, we find a friend.

The whispers of the past grow still,
In holy trust, we seek the will.
Each heartbeat echoes prayers profound,
In every soul, our light is found.

So come, dear child, to this embrace,
A sanctum of love, a sacred space.
In healing grace, we rise and soar,
Together united, forevermore.

Wings of Graceful Acceptance

Upon the winds, our spirits soar,
With open hearts, we seek the more.
Through trials faced, we learn to bend,
With wings of grace, our souls transcend.

In every challenge, wisdom waits,
A chance to meet our humble fates.
With gratitude, we learn to see,
The beauty found in being free.

Embrace the storm, let courage swell,
Through darkest nights, our stories tell.
In acceptance, burdens lift away,
A brighter dawn, a brand new day.

With every tear, a lesson learned,
The heart grows wise, its passion burned.
In love's embrace, we find our way,
With wings of light, we gently sway.

So spread your wings, dear child of grace,
Each moment cherished, time won't erase.
In gentle flight, our spirits blend,
With wings of love, forever mend.

The Alchemy of Healing Hearts

In sacred flame, the hearts ignite,
Transformed through love, we find our light.
The alchemy of soul's embrace,
In every tear, we seek the grace.

Through trials faced, rebirth is found,
In every wound, a holy sound.
The whispers of the ancients call,
To rise again, to not let fall.

In unity, the journey flows,
With humble hearts, our spirit grows.
In shadows cast, we learn to shine,
In love's sweet name, our souls align.

So let us gather, hand in hand,
And face the storms that life has planned.
In healing circles, hearts will mend,
Through love's embrace, the hope transcends.

In every heartbeat, magic stirs,
A gift of life, in all it blurs.
For in this space, we rise anew,
The alchemy of love is true.

Grace Restored

In stillness, grace descends,
A whisper soft and clear,
Reminding us of love,
That cast away all fear.

Hearts once heavy find their light,
In faith's embrace we stand,
With every tear now turned to joy,
As mercy holds our hand.

Through trials, we grow strong,
Our spirits rise anew,
In the warmth of His presence,
We find our journey true.

The light of hope shines bright,
Illuminating the way,
With footsteps firm we march,
Guided by love's display.

Let us sing of grace restored,
In praises, we unite,
For through His eternal love,
Our souls take joyful flight.

Beneath the Weight of Mercy

Beneath the weight of mercy,
Our burdens feel so light,
In shadows, we discover,
The promise of the night.

Each trial that we carry,
Is met with gentle grace,
As love pours down like raindrops,
In this holy space.

Hearts once filled with sorrow,
Now dance in joy's embrace,
For mercy flows like rivers,
We find our rightful place.

Forgiveness, sweet and tender,
Meets anger with a balm,
In every whispered prayer,
We nurture quiet calm.

Together in His mercy,
We rise above the storm,
With every step of kindness,
In love, we are reborn.

In the Shadow of Reconciliation

In the shadow of reconciliation,
We find our hearts entwined,
Breaking down the walls of old,
A new path we define.

Through struggle, we are molded,
A tapestry of grace,
With threads of understanding,
Our stories interlace.

From ashes we will rise,
With hope upon our lips,
In unity, we gather,
As love’s sweet hymn eclipses.

Each wound will find its healing,
There's beauty in the scar,
For by His light we journey,
Together, near and far.

In faith we bind our spirits,
To mend the broken ties,
For every heart’s redemption,
Is where true freedom lies.

The Path to Divine Patience

The path to divine patience,
Is paved with love's embrace,
In quiet moments waiting,
We find our sacred space.

Through trials, we are tempered,
Like silver in the flame,
Each lesson learned with honor,
We rise, we grow, we claim.

In the stillness, hear His voice,
Whispering to our souls,
Patience is the gift we share,
As time within Him rolls.

With every step of kindness,
We sow seeds of His grace,
A journey long and winding,
Yet filled with warm embrace.

Each moment’s fleeting essence,
Reflects His love divine,
With faith and strength beside us,
In patience, we align.

Ascending Through Betrayal

In shadows deep, hearts find the way,
Betrayal's sting can lead astray.
Yet through the pain, we rise anew,
Ascending heights with faithful view.

In sorrow's grasp, we seek the light,
The dawn will break, dispelling night.
Forgive the wounds that cut so deep,
In love's embrace, our spirits leap.

Each tear that falls, a seed is sown,
From ashes cold, our faith is grown.
Together strong, we bear the weight,
Unbroken souls, defying fate.

Through trials fierce, we stand as one,
Betrayal’s night will soon be done.
With open hearts, we move ahead,
On wings of hope, our spirits fed.

So lift your gaze, the sky will clear,
From darkness found, embrace the near.
In unity, our spirits soar,
Ascending high, forevermore.

Lanterns of Love on a Darkened Path

In twilight's hour, we seek the flame,
Lanterns of love, we call your name.
Through darkened paths, they softly glow,
Guiding our hearts where we must go.

When shadows creep, and doubt feels near,
Let love's light shine, dispel the fear.
With every step, we hold the hand,
Of those we cherish, a sacred band.

Through trials faced, our spirits blend,
In love's embrace, the wounds will mend.
With lanterns bright, we walk as one,
The journey shared, never undone.

In moments still, when silence reigns,
Our hearts unite through joy and pains.
With every flicker, every sigh,
The light of love will never die.

So let us walk, side by side,
With lanterns held, hearts open wide.
For on this path, through darkened night,
The love we share will guide our flight.

Resurrecting Bonds of Trust

In fractured hearts, we search for peace,
Resurrecting bonds that fear'd release.
Through trials faced, we heal the pain,
In trust restored, we rise again.

When doubt encroaches, we must hold fast,
To sacred ties that bind the past.
Each whispered truth, a bridge to mend,
In honesty, we find a friend.

Through storms that rage, and winds that howl,
We forge ahead, on faith we prowl.
A promise made, to lift and share,
With open hearts, we show we care.

In unity, our spirits blend,
With every bond that we defend.
Resurrect the trust, let love abound,
In every heartbeat, joy is found.

So take my hand, let's walk this way,
Resurrecting bonds for every day.
In love's embrace, our past we grace,
Together strong, we'll find our place.

The Healing Touch of Grace

In silent whispers, grace descends,
A healing touch, where sorrow ends.
Through trials faced, our hearts embrace,
In gentle hands, we find our place.

When burdens weigh, and spirits tire,
Grace comes in waves, a soothing fire.
In every moment, find the bliss,
The touch of grace, a sacred kiss.

With every step, let kindness reign,
Transcending anguish, easing pain.
In love's soft glow, we mend the soul,
The healing touch makes fractured whole.

Through darkest nights, and storms that pass,
We seek the light, the truth, the glass.
In grace, we rise, together stand,
In unity, we hold love's hand.

So let us shine, with hearts set free,
The healing touch, our legacy.
In every heart, let grace reside,
A tender peace, forever guide.

Covenant of Renewal

In the stillness, hearts awaken,
Promises of hope unspoken,
With each dawn, a chance to mend,
The soul's journey, Christ our friend.

Gathered in faith, we unite,
Casting shadows into light,
With grace's touch, we strive and climb,
Renewed in spirit, through all time.

Anchored deep in love's embrace,
In every trial, we find grace,
Bound by mercy's gentle call,
Together, we shall never fall.

Whispers of joy in the air,
Each moment, a sacred prayer,
Firm in our covenant, we stand,
Hand in hand, led by His hand.

As seasons change, His light remains,
In joys and struggles, love sustains,
Through trials passed, we forge ahead,
In the covenant, softly led.

Cultivating a Heart of Kindness

In the garden of our days,
Seeds of kindness softly graze,
Each act of love, a bloom that grows,
In tender hearts, compassion flows.

A smile shared, a hand extended,
In service, grace is unending,
Nurturing the souls around,
In kindness deep, true life is found.

With every word, we plant a seed,
In caring hearts, we meet the need,
Bridging gaps with gentle care,
Together, burdens we can share.

Through stormy seas and darkened skies,
Kindness shines, a sweet surprise,
Guided by a higher trust,
In love and hope, our spirits must.

So let us walk with humble hearts,
In every space, each life imparts,
As we cultivate, may grace align,
In kindness, let our souls entwine.

The Sacred Embrace of Healing

In whispered prayers, we seek His face,
The sacred gift of healing grace,
Brokenness laid bare, gently held,
In His embrace, our fears dispelled.

With every tear, a story shared,
In fellowship, our hearts prepared,
To touch the wounds of others' pain,
In love's soft light, we grow again.

Hearts intertwine, a holy bond,
Through trials faced and nights beyond,
Finding solace in each embrace,
In unity, we find our place.

With faith as anchor, hope our guide,
In every challenge, we abide,
Restoration flows like gentle streams,
As we uplift each other's dreams.

So let us be the hands of grace,
In every lost and lonely space,
For in the healing, love unfolds,
A sacred tale of joy retold.

Breathing Life into Broken Bonds

In the shadows, we often falter,
Yet love can mend what lies asunder,
With gentle breath, we speak restore,
Reviving hearts that yearn for more.

Through every crack, light finds a way,
In fractured ties, we choose to stay,
With kindness' balm, wounds start to heal,
In the embrace, our spirits reel.

Forgiveness flows like rivers wide,
Easing burdens, tearing pride,
In humble hearts, the promise sings,
Binding us with angel wings.

With faith ignited, hope renewed,
Our broken bonds, by love imbued,
Each step we take, together true,
In harmony, our spirits grew.

So let us breathe life into despair,
In unity, our love laid bare,
For every fracture, grace will find,
The beauty of a heart entwined.

Healing Waters of Compassion

In the stillness of the night,
Flow the waters pure and bright,
With each drop, a gentle grace,
Healing hearts in time and space.

Candles flicker, shadows dance,
In this sacred, soft expanse,
Let the sorrow wash away,
In the dawn of a new day.

Every tear a river free,
Washing wounds that cannot see,
Lift the spirit, mend the soul,
In compassion, we are whole.

From the depths, the spirits rise,
Underneath the vastest skies,
In the waters, hearts entwine,
Boundless love, a holy sign.

Feel the current pulsing strong,
A reminder of our song,
Together, we shall find our peace,
In the waters, love's release.

The Path to Reconciliation

In the shadows of despair,
There's a bridge beyond compare,
Step by step, we make our way,
Toward the light of a new day.

Voices whisper from the past,
Healing words that long will last,
In forgiveness, hearts unite,
Turning darkness into light.

Each small gesture, like a seed,
Grows into a sacred deed,
Planting roots in fertile ground,
In this truth, love will be found.

Clasping hands, we break the chains,
Through the losses, through the pains,
Every soul a shining star,
On this path, we've come so far.

Let us walk with gentle grace,
In each other, find our place,
Toward horizons, strong and clear,
Together, casting out all fear.

Love’s Whisper Through the Storm

When the tempest roars aloud,
And the skies are darkly shrouded,
There’s a whisper in the gale,
Promising we shall not fail.

In the chaos, find the calm,
Every heart is fueled with balm,
Holding tight to dreams we share,
In the storm, we find our prayer.

Raindrops fall like gentle tears,
Washing away all our fears,
Sun will shine when clouds are past,
Love’s embrace will hold us fast.

Through the thunder, through the night,
Hope emerges, bold and bright,
In the fury, we can stand,
Together, hand in hand.

As the winds begin to cease,
In our hearts, we feel the peace,
Love’s sweet whisper, soft and warm,
Guides us gently through the storm.

Embracing the Splintered Soul

In the brokenness, we find,
Pieces scattered, intertwined,
Cradling wounds with tender care,
In our hearts, we learn to share.

Like a puzzle, we belong,
In each fragment, echoes strong,
With each shard, we craft anew,
Healing light will guide us through.

Each story, a sacred thread,
Woven dreams in paths we've tread,
Embracing all that pain bestows,
In our midst, compassion grows.

Hold the splinters, cherish each,
For in love, we learn to teach,
In acceptance, we are whole,
Binding tight the splintered soul.

Through the tears, a river flows,
In our hearts, the journey glows,
And together, we shall rise,
With open hearts beneath the skies.

Milton Keynes UK
Ingram Content Group UK Ltd.
UKHW020043271124
451585UK00012B/1017